National Park Explorers

EVERGLADES

by Sara Gilbert

CREATIVE EDUCATION · CREATIVE PAPERBACKS

TABLE OF CONTENTS

Cypress trees can grow in standing water.

WELCOME TO EVERGLADES NATIONAL PARK!

Be careful! You might meet an alligator! They live
in these swamps and ponds.

The Everglades are in Florida. The area became a national park in 1947. It is a safe place for animals and plants to live.

★ Everglades National Park
▪ Florida

A great blue heron (above); a butterfly on a thistle (right)

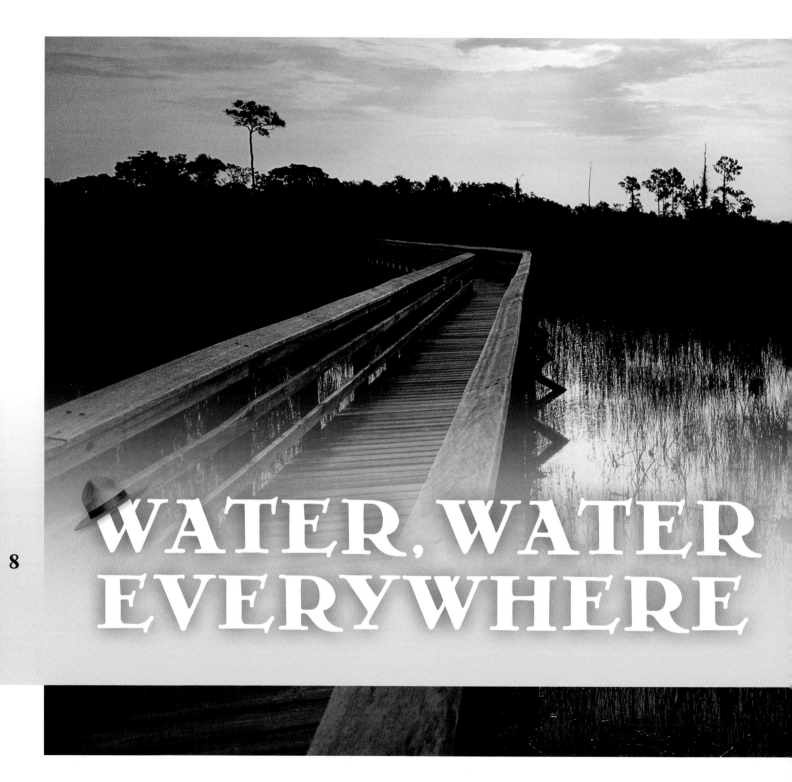

8

WATER, WATER EVERYWHERE

Almost everything is wet in the Everglades. Trails and bridges cross some of the **wetlands**. You can boat around other parts of the 1.5-million-acre (607,028 ha) park.

Watch out for West Indian manatees! These slow animals are called "sea cows."

A West Indian manatee (above); palmetto plants (right)

SAFE HAVEN

Many **endangered** animals live in the park. The Florida panther is a kind of cougar. There are fewer than 200 Florida panthers in the wild.

Alligators and crocodiles live near mangrove, cypress, and pine trees. A plant called lichen (*LYE-ken*) grows on the trees.

Red blanket lichen (below); alligators by a mangrove tree (right)

BY BOAT OR BIKE

More than one million people visit the Everglades every year. You can see the park by boat. You can hike or ride bikes on the trails. Visit the Everglades in the winter. It is still warm there then!

18 Take insect repellent and sunscreen. They will protect you from bugs and the sun. Bring water, too!

A dragonfly (above); marshes (right)

Do not forget your camera. You will want to take pictures of the animals you see—even the alligators!

The park is full of life, from great white egrets to alligators.

Activity

WHERE DOES THE WATER GO?

Materials needed:
Large sponge
Sheet-cake pan
Water

Step 1: Soak a sponge in water, and place it in the pan. The sponge is like the Everglades.

Step 2: Squeeze the sponge out into the pan. How much water comes out?

Step 3: Now let the sponge absorb some of the water from the pan. Squeeze it out in a sink. This is like when people take water out of the Everglades.

Step 4: Repeat step 3 until the water is gone. Think about what would happen if the Everglades dried up. What can be done to protect it?

Glossary

endangered — at risk of dying out, or disappearing from Earth

manatees — large, plant-eating animals that live in the water

wetlands — swamps, marshes, and other areas of land that are wet

Read More

George, Jean Craighead, and Wendell Minor. *Everglades*. New York: HarperCollins, 1997.

National Geographic. *National Geographic Kids National Parks Guide U.S.A.: The Most Amazing Sights, Scenes, and Cool Activities from Coast to Coast*. Washington, D.C.: National Geographic Society, 2012.

Websites

Kids Discover: National Parks

http://www.kidsdiscover.com/spotlight/national-parks-for-kids/
See pictures from the parks and learn more about their history.

WebRangers

http://www.nps.gov/webrangers/
Visit the National Park Service's site for kids to find fun activities.

Index

Published by Creative Education and Creative Paperbacks
P.O. Box 227, Mankato, Minnesota 56002 • Creative Education
and Creative Paperbacks are imprints of The Creative Company
www.thecreativecompany.us

Design and production by Christine Vanderbeek
Art direction by Rita Marshall
Printed in the United States of America

Photographs by Alamy (Frans Lanting Studio, Joan Gil, James
Schwabel), Corbis (Michael DeFreitas/Robert Harding World
Imagery, Scott Leslie/Minden Pictures, moodboard, Jim
Richardson, Galen Rowell, Phil Schermeister, Tim Tadder, Visuals
Unlimited), Dreamstime (Wisconsinart), Getty Images (Kick
Images), Shutterstock (Tarchyshnik Andrei, Alita Bobrov,
cretolamna, eAlisa, FloridaStock, Stephen B. Goodwin, JIANG
HONGYAN, iofoto, Eric Isselee, Alexey Kamenskiy, Philip Lange,
Larsek, LI CHAOSHU, pandapaw, Jason Patrick Ross)

Library of Congress Cataloging-in-Publication Data
Gilbert, Sara. • Everglades / by Sara Gilbert. • p. cm. — (National
park explorers) • *Summary*: A young explorer's introduction to
Florida's Everglades National Park, covering its wetlands landscape,
plants, animals such as West Indian manatees, and activities such as
boating. • Includes index. • ISBN 978-1-60818-631-0 (hardcover)
ISBN 978-1-62832-239-2 (pbk) • ISBN 978-1-56660-668-4
(eBook) • 1. Everglades National Park (Fla.)—Juvenile literature.
I. Title.

F317.E9G55 2016
975.9'39—dc23   2014048898

CCSS: RI.1.1, 2, 3, 4, 5, 6, 7, 10; RI.2.1, 2, 3, 5, 6, 7; RI.3.1, 3, 5, 7;
RF.1.1, 3, 4; RF.2.4

First Edition HC 9 8 7 6 5 4 3 2 1
First Edition PBK 9 8 7 6 5 4 3 2 1